GREEK
Myths and Legends

Retold by Anthony Masters

Illustrated by Andrew Skilleter

PETER BEDRICK BOOKS

NEW YORK

To Robina — as always with much love, A.M.
In memory of Pepper, A.S.

Published in the United States in 1999
by Peter Bedrick Books
a division of NTC/Contemporary
Publishing Group, Inc
4255 West Touhy Avenue
Lincolnwood (Chicago), Illinois 60646-1975 U.S.A.

Commissioning Editor: Dereen Taylor
Series Editor: Lisa Edwards
Series Design: The Design Works
Book Designer: Jean Wheeler
Production Controller: Carol Titchener

Masters, Anthony, 1940-
Greek Myths and legends / retold by Anthony Masters :
illustrated by Andrew Skilleter.
p.   cm.
Summary: A retelling of Greek Myths, including those about
Perseus and Medusa, Pandora's box, and the Golden Fleece.
ISBN 0-87226-609-5 (hc)
1. Mythology, Greek Juvenile literature. [1. Mythology, Greek.]
I. Skilleter, Andrew, ill. II. Title.
BL782.M335 2000
398.2'0938--dc21   99-27849
                                          CIP

Printed and bound in Portugal by Edições ASA

International Standard Book Number: 0-87226-609-5

99 00 01 02 03 15 14 13 12 11 10 9 8 7 6 5 4 3 2 1

CONTENTS

A pronunciation guide to all the
Greek names of people and places
featured in this book can be found
on page 45.

INTRODUCTION

The myths and legends of Ancient Greece are both mysterious and magical. I have retold them as the exciting, highly dramatic adventures that they really are. Each story takes us back to the dawn of time, with tales of gods and spirits, demons and disasters, giants and monsters, ghosts and battles, heroes and villains – the very essence of good and evil.

In ancient times, these stories helped people to understand the world around them – how the world was created, what happened to people when they died, and so on. This information was chiefly passed around by the spoken word, through the earliest storytellers.

The Ancient Greek poets had an imaginative way of describing this process – as if a bird was fluttering from one person's lips to another person's ears.

The reason we are able to enjoy these stories today is because they were passed down through generations of people.

They have probably changed considerably over time, rather like a game where a message is passed from person to person, becoming distorted and getting reinvented each time.

The five Greek myths and legends chosen for this book include the story of Perseus's battle with Medusa, a hideous monster with a cluster of hissing serpents for hair; Orpheus's tragic adventure in the Underworld; Daedalus, the first mortal to experiment with a flying machine; Pandora, accidentally releasing evil into the world, and Jason's courageous quest for the Golden Fleece.

Brooding over each story is the presence of the gods, who, far from being a source of comfort in this ever-changing mythical world, were as unpredictable as life itself.

ANTHONY MASTERS

PERSEUS AND MEDUSA

*"I'll bring you Medusa's head, if you like,"
said Perseus boastfully, draining the last
dregs of wine from his goblet.*

*The court was silent. No one had ever
succeeded in carrying out such a heroic and
difficult task.*

*"Why not?" suggested King Polydectes
in delight. "I'll hold you to that."*

*Now, as he made his preparations, Perseus was feeling distinctly
nervous. He must have been mad. But there was no way out. He would
have to travel to Cisthene, cut off the head of one of the monstrous
Gorgons and bring the thing back with him.*

*King Polydectes could hardly believe his good fortune. He had
little use for a Gorgon's head, but he knew that anyone foolhardy or
brave enough to make the attempt was very unlikely to come back
alive. The lair of the Gorgons was reputed to be a terrible place.*

*The king wanted Perseus out of his way. What better way for him
to meet his death than pitting his wits against the Gorgons?*

PERSEUS'S CHILDHOOD HAD BEEN DIFFICULT. He was the son of
Zeus, king of the gods, and Danaë, Princess of Argos, and he
should have had a happy boyhood. Unfortunately, his grandfather
Acrisius, King of Argos, discovered through an ancient prophecy that
his daughter's child would be the cause of his death. Panicking,

Acrisius locked both Danaë and Perseus in a chest and threw them into the sea.

Although they were rescued by a fisherman and taken to King Polydectes of Seriphus who gave them a home, this was not to be an end to their problems. King Polydectes was determined to marry Danaë. So far she had been able to refuse him and Danaë was confident that Perseus, her son, would always be there to protect her if the king became a nuisance. But when Perseus began to boast about Medusa, Polydectes seized his chance to get rid of him. The gods, however, were not prepared to let Polydectes send Perseus to his death in such an underhanded way and they lent Perseus some of their most prized possessions to help him. Hermes gave him his winged sandals; Hades his helmet of invisibility; Athene offered her shield, which was so highly polished that it looked like a mirror; and Hephaestus lent his sickle, which was made of diamonds.

Perseus felt a surge of confidence. He couldn't have been better prepared. With the aid of the magic sandals Perseus was able to run in the air with Athene acting as his guide to Cisthene to find the Gorgons. But he still had no idea what he would discover in the Gorgons' lair.

When he arrived in Cisthene, Perseus decided to take action at once. Trying to stay confident he approached the cave of the Gorgons. He knew that one of them – Medusa – had once been a beautiful maiden with the most magnificent head of hair. Unfortunately she had made the mistake of showing off to Athene, rather like Perseus had boasted to Polydectes. As a result, Athene changed Medusa into a hideous monster, her elegant ringlets now a cluster of hissing serpents. Anyone who looked into her eyes was immediately turned to stone. No one had survived the deadly stare so far. But then none of them had had the advantage of the gods' magical gifts.

As Perseus anxiously approached, he discovered the Gorgons' lair was part of a huge underground cave system that was as cold as death itself and pitch black. The entrance was guarded by the Graeae, who were the Gorgons' three sisters. When Perseus saw the hideous trio, he noticed that they only had one eye and one tooth between them. While two of the Graeae slept, the third took the eye and the tooth and stayed on guard. Once her duty watch was over, she would then wake one of her sisters and hand over the eye and the tooth.

Perseus wondered how he was going to get past the Graeae. Then he remembered his first gift – Hades's helmet of invisibility. Putting it on and vanishing from sight, he waited until one of the guard change-overs took place and then quickly slipped past. At the same time, Perseus managed to seize the eye and tooth.

He stole deeper into the cavern and at last came up on the three sleeping monsters known as the Gorgons. All around the cave were the stone figures of both humans and animals, and Perseus knew that he would meet the same fate if he so much as glanced into Medusa's eyes. But how could he kill Medusa without being able to see her? Perseus racked his brains and thought of the gods' magical gifts. Which one would serve him best?

Then he saw the flashing light of Athene's shield. Suppose he avoided facing Medusa by using the mirror-like surface to see exactly where she was sleeping? Gazing into the highly polished surface and remembering to reverse all his movements, Perseus drew out Hephaestus's diamond-studded sickle and began to search out Medusa. He had to attack her before she woke up and that could happen at any time. Concentrating deeply, Perseus checked the shield yet again. Then he swiftly closed in on her and slashed with the sickle.

Blood spurted everywhere as Medusa's head was severed, and where the liquid touched the ground it grew into the winged horse Pegasus that Athene trained and gave as a present to the Muses. Amazed at his good fortune, Perseus threw Medusa's head into a bag,

and offering up renewed thanks to Hermes for the loan of his winged sandals flew out of the cave.

On his way back home, Perseus passed over Africa and threw the Graeae's eye and tooth into Lake Tritonis, leaving the three sisters blind and defenseless forever. Medusa's head, however, was to come in surprisingly useful.

As night fell, Perseus became exhausted, and when he reached the western limit of the Earth where the sun sinks below the horizon, he decided he would have to take a rest. He landed in the Kingdom of Atlas. Atlas was one of the Titans, condemned for his part in the rebellion against the gods to support the sky on his shoulders for ever. Despite his amazing task, Atlas was a forbidding sight. He was also known to be very possessive of his orchards full of golden fruit.

Unfortunately, Perseus made the mistake of boasting again. He told Atlas that he should be treated with respect as he had conquered

Medusa. If that wasn't enough, he told him that his father was king of the gods. Atlas, however, was not impressed. It all sounded extremely unlikely to him. Then he suddenly became uneasy, remembering an ancient prophecy which had warned him that a son of Zeus would one day come to rob him of his golden apples.

With all of the sky to support he was in a difficult position to defend his orchards, but Atlas managed to use one hand to beat off Perseus, shouting, "Begone! Neither your false claims of glory nor parentage shall protect you."

Perseus found that the giant was too strong for him, even if he was using only one hand. Then he had an idea. "Since you value my friendship so little, why don't you accept a present?" Perseus shouted, bringing Medusa's head out of his bag.

When Atlas's gaze met her dead eyes he was immediately turned to stone. His hair and beard became forests, his arms and shoulders cliffs, his head the summit of a mountain and his bones rocks. As Perseus watched, the giant was slowly transformed into the Atlas mountains in North Africa whose peaks still seem to support the sky.

Perseus's next landing was equally dangerous. Gazing down at the North African coast as he soared through the air, Perseus saw a beautiful young woman chained to a rock. She was so pale and motionless as she stood there that had it not been for her hair moving in the breeze and the tears flowing down her cheeks, Perseus would have taken the girl for a marble statue.

Moved by her plight he landed beside her, demanding to know why she had been chained. Sobbing bitterly, she told him her name was Andromeda and she was bait for a sea-monster. Her mother Cassiopeia had been sufficiently vain and foolish to boast that her own beauty was far greater than that of the daughters of the sea nymphs, and, as a result, Poseidon, king of the sea, had been very angry.

Andromeda's terrified parents knew Poseidon would have to be offered a sacrifice. Now the innocent Andromeda was tied to a rock, waiting for the hungry sea-monster while her parents looked on helplessly from above.

Suddenly an enormous wave thundered in and the monster's fierce eyes glared out from the spray. Perseus turned to Andromeda's parents and demanded their daughter's hand in marriage if he succeeded in killing the monster. They agreed immediately.

Once again, Perseus knew he was completely dependent on the magic of the gods. Would it work yet one more time?

Using his magic sandals, Perseus bounded into the air, landing on the monster's back and seizing the huge neck. Now that the monster was unable to turn its head, Perseus was able to plunge his diamond-studded sickle through the scales and kill it.

But Perseus's troubles were not over. At his wedding feast, Andromeda's ex-suitor, Phineus, burst in with a group of supporters. He was furious at having lost Andromeda, despite the fact that he had done nothing to protect her while she was bound to the rock. In a rage, Phineus hurled his javelin at Perseus but fortunately it missed him. Hand-to-hand fighting broke out amongst the guests – a battle which was abruptly ended by Perseus rummaging in his bag and holding up Medusa's head.

Phineus's supporters were immediately turned to stone, frozen as they fought. In the deep and horrified silence, Phineus called aloud to his friends, but there was no reply. Desperately he touched them, but their bodies were dry and hard and lifeless.

Falling on his knees, Phineus pleaded for his own life, promising Perseus all his money and possessions as well as Andromeda. But Perseus knew his rival could never be trusted.

"No weapon shall touch you but you'll be preserved here as a memorial of these events," he said, holding up Medusa's head yet again, and Phineus became a kneeling statue, his hands outstretched.

Perseus lifted Andromeda into his arms and they soared away from the ruins of the marriage feast, flying home to Seriphus. But when he arrived, Perseus had to face yet another problem. In his absence, King Polydectes had tried to force his mother to marry him and Danaë had taken refuge in the temple of Athene, which Polydectes and his personal guards had surrounded. When Perseus flew over their heads and saw the terrible danger threatening his mother, he decided to use Medusa's head yet again. As Polydectes and his guards looked up to gasp at the sight of Perseus and Andromeda soaring above them in the sky, Perseus pulled out Medusa's head and immediately turned them all into a circle of stones.

Then Perseus set out from Seriphus with Andromeda to found a new kingdom, but before he went, Perseus returned to the gods all the magic objects they had lent him: the winged sandals, the helmet of invisibility, the diamond-studded sickle and the glittering mirror-shield. He also made Athene a present of Medusa's head, which she placed as a protective device on the front of her mirror-shield.

After many years Perseus, Danaë and Andromeda returned to Argos but King Acrisius was not at home. He had been warned that the trio were on their way and, remembering the ancient prophecy that Perseus would be the cause of his death, had fled to Larissa in Thessaly, in a vain attempt to protect himself. But Perseus followed his grandfather to Larissa and "accidentally" killed him with a badly aimed discus.

When Perseus died he was given a hero's welcome on Mount Olympus, the highest mountain in Greece, the home of the gods.

ORPHEUS AND EURYDICE

Eurydice was swimming in the River Peneus. She allowed the cool water to carry her along into a large pool where she floated, completely relaxed, unaware she was being watched.

Aristaeus, a wandering teacher, had seen her and was attracted to her beauty.

He plunged into the pool but she swam swiftly to the bank and fled. Aristaeus pursued her, and in her haste to escape, Eurydice trod on a poisonous snake and was bitten in the foot. When Aristaeus caught up with her he was appalled to see that she lay lifeless on the ground.

Hades, king of the Underworld, instantly dispatched Death to collect her, and by the time word reached her husband, Orpheus, Eurydice had vanished. The dead were invisible to mortal eyes and Orpheus began to search the whole of Greece for her, playing his lyre in the vain hope that its music would bring Eurydice back to him.

ORPHEUS WAS A FAMOUS MUSICIAN who had been taught to play the lyre by his father, Apollo, the sun god. Calling Eurydice's name, singing and playing her favorite music and songs, he roamed the land until, at last, Hermes, messenger of the gods, took pity on him and told him where she had been taken.

Grief-stricken but determined not to give up, Orpheus decided to descend to the Underworld and the regions of the dead to try and

bring Eurydice back. Clambering down a dark tunnel at the back of a cave and still clutching his lyre, Orpheus eventually arrived at the banks of the Acheron, one of the rivers of the Underworld.

Orpheus played his lyre to Charon, the dreaded boatman who ferried the souls of the dead to the judgement seat of Hades. Bewitched and enchanted by the music, Charon rowed Orpheus across the river.

The gate to the kingdom of Hades was guarded by Cerberus, the three-headed watchdog. Each of his necks bristled with snakes. Barking fiercely and showing his enormous fangs, Cerberus guarded Hades against human intruders from the upper world. Few had succeeded in passing Cerberus, but so exquisite was the lullaby which Orpheus played on his lyre that he was able to lull Cerberus to sleep.

When Orpheus reached the dark throne of Hades and his queen, Persephone, he paused, trembling. He knew everything that mattered to him, the very meaning of life itself, hung in the balance. Singing more beautifully than he had ever done before, Orpheus explained the reason for his mission, pleading for the return of his beloved Eurydice whose precious life had been brought to such an untimely end. So beautiful and moving was the music that many of the dead wept.

Orpheus was a man of singular strength and purpose. He had been one of Jason's Argonauts and was no stranger to difficulties. Orpheus's determination soon won over the dead hearts of those in the Underworld. In fact, for a brief moment, he brought the misery of Hades to a halt. The cheeks of the Furies, the three monstrous sisters who supervised the torments of the wicked, were wet with tears. The blazing wheel on which the criminal Ixion was strapped stopped turning and Sisyphus, perpetually pushing an enormous boulder up a hill, actually paused to listen.

The Underworld had never been more moved by the plight of a mortal man. Persephone immediately wanted to help and even Hades finally gave in and called for Eurydice. Orpheus couldn't believe that

he had actually won her back as he watched his grey ghost of a wife emerge from the new arrivals in the Underworld and walk towards him, limping with her snake-bitten foot.

As Orpheus began to sing again Hades cried iron tears and promised that Orpheus could lead Eurydice back to the upper world. There was, however, one condition and if it was broken Eurydice would return to the Underworld forever. The condition was that Orpheus must not look back until he had reached Earth's surface. He readily agreed, for the problem seemed simple enough to avoid. He would never, ever look back.

Hermes, the messenger of the gods, was given the task of leading Orpheus and Eurydice on the slow and exhausting climb back to the upper world. Slowly, Orpheus's confidence grew. He hadn't looked back and he was sure that, in her turn, Eurydice was following him.

They walked in silence until at last they could just make out the light of the upper world piercing the gloom of the Underworld. Orpheus was so relieved to see the light after the sombre shades of the dead that he desperately wanted to turn round to make sure Eurydice was following.

Forgetting that this was the very last thing he should do, Orpheus turned. Eurydice was a few paces behind him and Hermes a few paces in front. Immediately, Orpheus realized from Eurydice's terrified expression how careless he had been. He had broken the condition. Orpheus glanced back at Hermes who was standing with a grim smile on his grey features.

Surely he wouldn't lose Eurydice for this quick backward glance? It was nothing. Just a little slip. Just a glimpse, that was all. Hades wouldn't have noticed – even if Hermes had. Orpheus decided to keep going, to pretend he had never glanced back.

But Hermes walked slowly towards him. His expression was steely. "You looked back," he said.

"I didn't."

"You looked back," persisted Hermes. "You broke the condition."

Orpheus began to argue fiercely with Hermes.

"Look behind you," said the messenger of the gods.

"I can't."

"You can now."

Orpheus wheeled round to see Eurydice weeping. She stretched out her arms to embrace him and he did the same, running towards her until he was running into nothing at all. Eurydice had become invisible. She was dead again, a victim of his own carelessness. Hermes was leading her back to the Underworld.

"Farewell," Eurydice whispered.

The word was like a sigh in his ears.

Orpheus was determined not to give up. He would return to the Underworld and plead with Hades to give him one final chance. He wandered the tunnels and caves of the entrance to the Underworld for seven days, calling Eurydice's name until he was hoarse. He played the sweetest music which echoed mournfully in the empty caverns.

Finally, he reached Charon. "Please take me across the river," he begged him. "I've *got* to find Eurydice."

"You've had your chance," replied the old man angrily. "And you're not getting a second one."

Desperately Orpheus sang and played to him, but the boatman still refused to row him across the river. Orpheus stayed on the bank for another seven days, pleading not only with Charon but with the powers of darkness themselves. Again and again Orpheus begged the

old ferryman to row him across the river, but he refused, deaf this time to the sweet music Orpheus played on his lyre.

Orpheus remained on the brink of the Underworld for many more days without either food or sleep. He sang his complaints to the rocks and the mountains, but although he melted the hearts of wandering tigers Orpheus did not move Hades. Now he knew for certain he would not be given a second chance.

The most appalling memories of his visit to the Underworld filled Orpheus's mind, and as he sat on the banks of the river he remembered sweetmeats being snatched from the mouths of the hungry. Other victims had huge rocks suspended over their heads, always threatening to fall, keeping them in a state of constant fear. Eventually, Orpheus approached Charon and told him about the terrible visions that tortured him.

"You should have listened to Hades. Didn't he tell you to drink from the waters of the River Lethe before leaving the Underworld? That would have rubbed out all memory of the souls in torment."

But Orpheus hadn't remembered anything he had been told. He could only recall his quest for Eurydice who he had lost so carelessly at the very last moment.

Orpheus stumbled back to the upper world, his mind still tormented by visions of the Underworld and the unbearable loss of Eurydice. He went to live high up in an isolated hermit's cave on Mount Pangaeum.

Soon, other mortals realized that Orpheus had not only achieved the miraculous task of entering the Underworld – but also of leaving it. As a result, groups of young men began to make pilgrimages to his lonely cave to sit at Orpheus's feet, learning the secrets of the grave.

As he told his stories, as the hellish visions festered in his mind, Orpheus continuously saw Eurydice's unearthly form walking towards him, delighted to be rescued. They could have been so happy. He had let her down badly. He never sought the company of other women.

Then, a group of Thracian women, tired of being ignored by Orpheus, vowed to take their revenge on him for his churlishness. Finding Orpheus asleep one day, they crept up on him.

"This is the man who despises us," yelled one of the Thracian women, and threw a javelin at him.

Orpheus's lyre, however, began to play by itself, and so moving was the sound that the weapon lost momentum and fell harmlessly at his feet. The same happened to the stones they threw.

The Thracian women wondered how they could defeat the magical lyre. Then they had an idea. The Thracian women began to scream, drowning the sound of the music. When their screaming was at its height they stoned Orpheus again. This time the missiles found their mark and were soon covered in his blood. The women then tore him limb from limb, screaming hysterically as they did so. The lyre, its music drowned, began to play a grief-stricken lament, as the Thracian women threw Orpheus's head and later his lyre into the River Hebrus. The lyre floated, murmuring sad music, and the banks of the river echoed with the tragic sound.

Orpheus's head and lyre floated to the island of Lesbos where the head was buried, but Apollo placed the lyre amongst the stars. Orpheus's spirit was taken over the River Styx by Charon and into the Underworld where at last he was reunited with Eurydice. Now they roam the Elysian Fields together, the groves where the happy dead live, far from the dark realms inhabited by those condemned to eternal torment.

Sometimes Eurydice leads on their long walks. Sometimes Orpheus. When he is in the lead, Orpheus often turns round to glance at his dearly loved wife. At last he knows that he will no longer be required to pay such a terrible penalty for a single backward glance.

THE BIRDMEN

Daedalus was building two flying machines, one for himself and the other for his beloved son Icarus. First of all he collected feathers and pieced them together, beginning with the smallest and gradually adding larger ones. Then he threaded the larger feathers together and waxed the smaller ones, shaping them into a gentle curve — just like the wings of a bird.

Soon, he and Icarus were going to escape from Crete and become the first men on Earth to fly. But he was very nervous. Would the feathers support their weight? Even if they did, Daedalus was acutely aware that if they flew too high, their bodies would be scorched by the heat of the sun. If they flew too low they could get weighed down by damp air. Just one mistake Daedalus reckoned, and the feathers could loosen, then they would plunge to their deaths.

ONCE, DAEDALUS AND KING MINOS OF CRETE had been friends. A famous architect and inventor, Daedalus had created palaces, intricate machines and huge ships for transporting grain. He had also invented an underwater ram, in the shape of a bird's beak, that was fixed to Cretan warships, giving them a terrifying reputation in battle. But without doubt his most famous creation was the Labyrinth.

This was an amazing construction, with winding passages and endless turnings that led nowhere. The maze had no beginning and no

end, and was specially built to contain the dreaded Minotaur, a monster that had a bull's head and a human body.

Although King Minos and Daedalus were partners in the creation of the Labyrinth, they had soon begun to distrust each other for Daedalus knew that King Minos had a terrible secret. The Minotaur was the child of Minos's wife Pasiphaë who had angered the god of the sea Poseidon. As revenge, he made her fall in love with a magnificent white bull and she gave birth to the Minotaur.

Each year, boys and girls were sent from Athens to Crete as tribute. The youngsters were driven into the Labyrinth and left to roam the maze, desperately trying to find a way out. But they simply exhausted themselves in the web of passages until they heard the echoing roar of the Minotaur. Then they were eaten alive.

At long last, it happened that the hero Theseus, himself a prince of Athens, volunteered to be one of the victims. He wanted to try to end his people's suffering by killing the Minotaur. Aided by the King's daughter, Ariadne, he eventually succeeded.

Convinced that Daedalus was involved in the murder of the Minotaur, King Minos imprisoned him and his son Icarus in a tower. They managed to escape by using knotted sheets to lower themselves to the ground. Daedalus now realized that in order to avoid capture, he and Icarus had to leave the country as quickly as possible. But King Minos was keeping a strict watch on all the ports and refusing to allow any ship to sail without carefully searching it. The only means of escape was to fly.

The building of the flying machines was Daedalus's greatest test as an inventor. He knew it would not be long before their hiding place was discovered, so he had to work fast.

Despite the haste, Daedalus carried out the difficult work of construction very carefully indeed. Icarus acted as his helper, running to gather up feathers that blew away or handling the wax, working it with his fingers. Sometimes he played and got in the way; other times he just watched. He trusted his father completely. Wasn't he the greatest inventor in the world? Soon they would both be flying as high as the birds, soaring away from the scheming King Minos.

Daedalus harnessed his son with his wings and taught him how to use them, just like a bird might have taught its young. The eager boy learned very quickly – it wasn't long before Daedalus was satisfied that Icarus was going to be able to manage his flying machine. But Daedalus was still terrified of the terrible danger he and his son faced.

"Icarus – you've *got* to keep at a certain height, not too high and not too low. If you fly too low the dampness of the sea will clog up your wings and if you fly too high the heat of the sun will melt them. Keep close to me. If you don't you'll be in serious danger."

Icarus nodded and promised he would do exactly as his father

instructed. But Daedalus knew his son could be a daredevil. He wept as he fitted the wings to his son's shoulders and his hands shook. What if something went wrong? What if he had miscalculated his measurements? Suppose his latest great invention suddenly fell to bits? But it was impossible to test-fly the machines for a long period with King Minos's guards searching for them day and night. They had to fly now – or be executed.

Daedalus was still horribly aware of the risk they were taking, but Icarus reassured his father, promising to keep near him at all times. So, without any further delay, Daedalus soared up into the air currents, signalling Icarus to follow. At once, they both experienced a great rush of elation. The invention worked beautifully and they were going to escape. What was more, they would go down in history as the first mortal men to fly. The gods would be amazed!

The air was warm and welcoming and its shifting currents carried both Daedalus and Icarus away with ease. They flew over the Labyrinth and later King Minos's palace, cheering as they did so.

So this is flying, thought Icarus. It was certainly the greatest experience he had ever had – how he would boast about it. But would anyone believe him? He would have to keep his wings when they arrived, and hope that his father would let him use them again.

As they moved through the air, birds passed Daedalus and Icarus. The gulls and cormorants gazed at them startled, more than a little afraid of their huge and majestic rivals who flew a little awkwardly at first, but seemed to be getting more practiced by the minute.

When Daedalus looked back he could see Icarus following his flight path, obeying him exactly as he had so solemnly promised to do. The sun had burst through the clouds and bathed them in its warm golden glow. As they flew, Daedalus and Icarus were a truly amazing sight. The shepherd leaned on his staff to watch the birdmen and the farmer stopped his work to gaze up at what he was sure was a miracle created by the gods. Gradually the news was passed to a furious King Minos, who knew at once that his subjects were not watching gods but the escaping Daedalus and Icarus.

As the sun grew warmer, Icarus gained in confidence and became so excited that he forgot his father's warnings and began to swoop about, climbing higher and higher towards the blazing heat of the sun.

All at once, under the sun's fierce rays, the wax in Icarus's wings began to melt. Icarus made desperate fluttering movements with his arms, but there were no more feathers left to hold him up in the air. Icarus plunged down into the sea at enormous speed, hitting the surface and disappearing beneath the water.

Daedalus couldn't take in what had happened. He hadn't seen his son fall and kept calling his name. Then, to his horror, he saw feathers floating on the heaving waves. Suddenly Icarus's body surfaced, drifting in towards land with the tide.

Stricken with grief, Daedalus began to descend, bitterly regretting that he had ever become an inventor. The worst had happened. He should have known Icarus would get over confident. He should have flown behind him, watching his every move.

Daedalus landed, and in despair, pulled his beloved son from the heaving waves. He buried him in a land that he named Icaria in memory of his child.

Heartbroken, he flew on to Sicily where he built a temple to Apollo and hung up his flying machine as an offering to the god. He never wanted to see his wings again.

King Minos, however, was still determined to take his revenge

and, besides that, a man of Daedalus's talents was a potential threat at the court of any rival ruler. The king knew that despite his bitter grief, the great inventor could never resist a problem. So King Minos set sail in his royal ship, carrying with him a shell. Every time he landed he made a public announcement that he would heavily reward anyone who could pass a thread through the shell without breaking it.

When King Minos arrived in Sicily, Daedalus was unable to resist the challenge, although he had no idea who was behind it.

Taking the shell, Daedalus spread honey on the outside, bored a hole in the closed end and carefully inserted an ant which was tied with a silken thread. The ant then ran through the shell to find the honey. King Minos knew that at last he had found his enemy. No one else could have been as ingenious as that. It *must* be Daedalus.

The king of Sicily was horrified by the arrival of the Minoan fleet in his harbor. Knowing that he was outnumbered he agreed to give Daedalus up. However, before Daedalus's arrest took place, Minos was offered the traditional hospitality bath organized by his host's daughters — a bath that was to prove fatal.

Over the years, Daedalus had made the Sicilian princesses many wonderful toys. If he was executed they would miss his inventions terribly so the princesses asked Daedalus how they could help.

Once again, he had an ambitious plan. Working extremely quickly, he laid a pipe through the roof of the bath house. Then Daedalus and the princesses poured boiling water down the pipe and King Minos was scalded to death.

Now that he was free from persecution, Daedalus spent the rest of his life in Sicily, distracting himself from the loss of his son by continuing to create the most amazing inventions.

When Daedalus died, he was taken into Olympus and joined the workshop of Hephaestus, the god of craftwork.

PANDORA'S BOX

Hermes, the winged messenger of the gods, had left a large box at the home of Pandora and her husband Epimetheus. He had given strict instructions that it should not be opened. But there the box was, standing in the corner of the room, the sunlight playing mysteriously on its surface.

Pandora's curiosity was at its breaking point. What possible harm would it do to open the thing? Several times she had asked Epimetheus if she could untie the golden cord that bound the lid, but each time he had refused, pointing out that Hermes trusted them to obey him.

Pandora, however, grew more and more frantic. What could possibly be inside that was so precious? So secret?

EPIMETHEUS WATCHED PANDORA ANXIOUSLY. She was the very first woman to live on Earth and had been created in Heaven specially to be his wife. Each of the gods had contributed towards her outstanding qualities, but Epimetheus couldn't entirely forget his brother Prometheus's warning. Pandora could have been sent to punish them for stealing fire from Heaven to give to humankind.

Epimetheus had been given the job of creating a human. He had to provide this person, along with all the other creatures on Earth, with gifts necessary for survival. He had given claws to one creature,

wings to another, shells to a third. But when it came to human beings, who had to be superior to them all, Epimetheus found he had run out of gifts. In desperation he had turned to his brother Prometheus, who, ever quick-witted, had secretly lit his torch from the sun.

Returning to Earth Prometheus had given humans the stolen gift of fire, which made them superior to all other animals but thoroughly enraged Zeus, king of the gods. Was it a coincidence that Pandora was Zeus's gift to Epimetheus?

Becoming more and more apprehensive, Epimetheus tried to warn Pandora about the box, explaining patiently that on no account was she to open it.

"We don't know why Hermes left it there," he persisted. "But he particularly said not to go near it. There must be a good reason."

"What could that be?" Pandora wondered, still staring at the box which was quite large and made of iron with a hinged lid. The box, would be so easy to open, she thought. It wasn't even locked, just secured with the golden cord.

"I can see you aren't convinced by what I've said," Epimetheus told his wife. "But I've got to trust you to do as I say."

Pandora knew that her husband had set her a test of obedience. But Pandora didn't feel obedient. Who was Epimetheus to give her orders? Pandora hated being dutiful.

Pandora lay in bed beside Epimetheus and tried to sleep, but she couldn't stop thinking about the box. Then she heard a strange sound and tried to work out what it could be. At last she realized that she was listening to a whispering that was gradually getting louder, although she couldn't make out what the words were. Pandora felt compelled to go nearer and listen.

She got out of bed, went over to the box and sat down, pressing her ear against the cold metal. The golden cord touched the side of her face. It felt soft and warm and inviting. Pandora knew how easy it would be to untie the knot and pull the cord away.

The whispering was even louder now, and there was rustling and what she thought was an agitated breathing, as if a large crowd had been lured into the box and kept prisoner. Suddenly Pandora started as she felt a gentle but firm hand on her shoulder. She looked up into Epimetheus's angry eyes and began to shake.

"Why did you disobey me?" he demanded.

"I haven't," she replied. "The box is still shut."

"I caught you just in time," he accused her.

"I was only listening. That's all. Can't you hear the whispering?"

Epimetheus shook his head. "I don't want to hear. Can't you leave the thing alone? If only Hermes would come and take this wretched box away." But he knew that they were both being tested, and despite her many gifts Pandora had a fatal flaw - curiosity.

They went back to bed and Epimetheus pretended to sleep, watching Pandora through half-closed eyes, determined not to let her out of his sight for a minute. But after a long struggle he couldn't keep his eyes open any longer and drifted away into deep sleep.

Pandora stiffened beside him. Now was her chance. She *had* to take it. Life would be unbearable if she didn't.

Pandora tiptoed across to the box, turning round every now and then to make absolutely sure that Epimetheus wasn't setting a trap for her or hadn't suddenly woken up. But the trap had already been set for her by the gods and she was heading straight for trouble.

Pandora stood staring down at the box. The whispering was louder, and now there was a scrabbling sound as if a huge army of tiny people was trying to get out. For a moment Pandora hesitated, and then began to try and undo the golden cord. As she struggled to undo the knot, she continued to glance back at Epimetheus. Once or twice he groaned in his sleep. But he didn't wake.

Pandora's stiff, cold fingers picked and pried at the knot until slowly it began to loosen. The cord slid off the box. Pandora rose to her feet trembling. Couldn't she just retie the knot and go back to bed? But she had come so far now that she knew she had to carry on.

The box seemed to quiver with life and the whispering was all around her now, sounding so loud in her ears that she could hardly bear it any longer. Slowly Pandora pulled open the clasp and lifted the lid. As she did so, a feeling of dread seized her. What *had* she done?

A huge cloud rose from the box and the whispering became a vicious buzzing sound as dozens of brown, winged little creatures hovered in the air like moths.

For a moment Pandora gaped at them, but when they sensed her terrified presence they dived on her in a thick swarm. Immediately she felt pricks and stings all over her body. Pandora beat at the tiny creatures with her hands, but she could do nothing.

Epimetheus, awakened by the sound, jumped out of bed. "What have you done?" he yelled.

"I've opened the box," Pandora screamed as she was stung and pricked and stung again. Never had she been so afraid.

The swarm of vicious little moth-like creatures then attacked Epimetheus, and although he tried to beat them off they continued to torment him as he struggled to force down the lid of the box. Eventually he managed to slam it shut, although Epimetheus was sure he was too late and the box was empty.

"You idiot," he yelled at Pandora. "You're so shallow and weak. You couldn't stop yourself, could you?"

But rather than being sorry, Pandora blazed back at him in red-hot fury, "Why shouldn't I have opened it? I'll not be told what to do by you or even Hermes. If there were dozens of boxes I'd have opened them all."

As they argued and shouted, the brown, winged creatures soared out of the door in a thick cloud. Soon Pandora and Epimetheus could

hear screams as they attacked the rest of the village, and at last Pandora began to feel sorry for what she had done.

"I didn't mean to do such harm," she wept.

Epimetheus, still angry but now feeling sorry for his wife's guilt and pain, put his arm round her. "Let's go and look outside," he suggested, secretly terrified of what they might find.

It was an appalling sight. From the village down to the river, men and women and children were arguing and fighting. They were being as cruel to each other as they could possibly be. Envy, spite and revenge burned in everyone's heart.

"How has all this happened?" asked Pandora, trying to pretend to herself that she couldn't possibly be responsible for all this suffering.

"You let evil out of the box," replied Epimetheus grimly.

In the valley the river was breaking its banks. Its dark waters were evil. Modesty, truth and honor had disappeared, and in their place came fraud and cunning and violence and greed.

The valley, which had once been cultivated by everyone, was being divided off into strips, claimed by and argued over by the inhabitants who soon began killing each other.

Shaken, miserable and horrified, Epimetheus and Pandora returned indoors to gaze at the closed box.

Then they heard a voice.

It was coming from the box.

"Let me out," it said.

"Don't go near," yelled Epimetheus, and Pandora stood staring at him, not knowing what to do. Was it another trap? Could she unleash more demons?

"Let me out," repeated the voice, but still neither of them moved.

"Let me out," came the voice yet again. "I am Hope. Everyone needs Hope."

Slowly and hesitantly, Pandora began to walk towards the box, but Epimetheus grabbed her arm.

"Don't go near the thing," he shouted at her. "You know it's a trap. You could let out even more evil than you have already."

"Surely there can't be anything worse in there than what we've seen outside?" Pandora replied doubtfully.

She pulled away from Epimetheus, opened the clasp and lifted the lid of the metal box once more.

At first the interior seemed empty. Then Pandora saw something fluttering up towards her and she stepped back in fear. Could this single creature be an even greater evil masquerading as Hope?

A white moth flew out and began to descend on both of them in turn. But instead of attacking, the moth healed their wounds. Epimetheus and Pandora grew calmer.

The white moth fluttered out of the door into the dark chaos of the world outside. Pandora and Epimetheus followed, praying that Hope would be able to banish the evil Pandora had released.

Outside, the fighting, arguing and shouting amongst the people ceased. The white moth flew towards the river and the evil flood trickled to a halt, the dark water lying on the fields.

Pandora and Epimetheus could hear a sweet singing in the air as the birds began their dawn chorus. The pale faces of the warring people looked up at Hope in relief. Although many of them continued to quarrel, a few laid down their weapons, and while some people remained ill, others slowly recovered.

"I haven't spoilt everything," Pandora pleaded. 'At least I had the courage to release Hope."

Epimetheus was silent.

Jason and the Golden Fleece

The new ship was an incredible sight. The Argo lay moored in a natural harbor on the shores of Thessaly, and fifty men sitting at their oars gazed up at Jason who stood in the prow.

"To the Golden Fleece," he shouted, draining the goblet of wine. "To our quest."

The crew cheered. They were all young and strong and were looking forward to the adventure ahead of them, hardly giving a thought to its dangers.

PELIAS, JASON'S UNCLE, had been ruling Thessaly until Jason came of age. When Jason was old enough to claim the throne, Pelias had the crafty idea of suggesting a glorious mission, secretly hoping that Jason would never return.

Fired with enthusiasm for the quest, Jason had sent out an invitation to the bravest young men in Greece. Now, at last, they had all arrived, each wanting to be a hero. They were called the Argonauts after the name of their ship.

The *Argo* sailed with the tide, the crew pulling at the oars to shouted instructions, the rhythm building, their muscles bulging as they rowed towards the open sea. The ship's course took her towards the island of Lemnos and then to Mysia and eventually to Thrace. There, Jason landed and spoke to the wise man Phineus while the crew took on fresh water and supplies.

Now the real dangers of the voyage were beginning and Phineus told Jason the best course to take through the magical, dangerous Clashing Islands. But, despite all Phineus's warnings, once the *Argo* arrived at the entrance to the Euxine Sea, the Argonauts still froze with horror. The sight was terrifying.

Directly in front of them were two small rocky islands, floating on the surface of the sea. They were heaving up and down in the water, sending spray flying and waves rolling to and fro.

Then, without any warning, the islands hurtled towards each other with a crashing and grinding of rock. Jason and the Argonauts knew all too well that if they were caught between them, the ship and its crew would be crushed immediately.

Phineus, however, had given Jason the gift of a dove which would show him a way through. Stroking its head, Jason released the bird and the Argonauts watched with total concentration, poised to start rowing at any moment.

The islands had drawn apart again, violently churning up the water. Then they suddenly began to travel back towards each other at an incredible speed and, for a moment, Jason thought the dove would be caught between the two as they clashed together again.

Then the Argonauts gave a cheer. The dove had passed through safely, losing only a few of her tail feathers. It was a miraculous escape. Could they do the same?

Knowing they only had a few minutes safe passage as the churning islands floated away from each other in a rain of loose rock, the Argonauts rowed with desperate strength towards the gap. They were terrified that at any moment the islands would plunge forward and trap them.

Now they were between the rocky outcrops, rowing furiously. Tense, sweating, muscles aching, hearts pounding, faces set, Jason and his crew prayed they would get through the gap unharmed.

All too soon they could hear the roaring of the waters and knew that the islands were hurtling towards each other yet again. They could feel cold spray, hear the rumbling of loose rock. The crew was bent double over the oars, straining, finding extra strength, determined not to be crushed.

As the islands bore down on them Jason forced himself to look up, watching the immensity of the speeding rocky cliffs. He was sure that it was too late and they had misjudged the split-second timing.

"Pull," Jason yelled at the Argonauts. "In the name of the gods – pull on your oars!"

The crew gave a ferocious cry, stretched their aching muscles again and the *Argo* shot through the gap. As she did so she began to vibrate. Had the ship been hit?

Jason raced back along the length of the violently shaking ship. To his relief the only damage was a faintly grazed stern. He gave a great shout of triumph as rock broke into the water behind them. The noise was deafening. The dove soared above them and then flew on towards the horizon.

The Argonauts rowed along the shore until on the eastern side of the sea they eventually arrived at the kingdom of Colchis where the Golden Fleece was reputed to hang in a grove of trees consecrated to Mars, the god of war. It was guarded by a dragon who never slept.

The Colchian king, Ætes, agreed to give up the fleece if Jason passed some tests which were cunningly devised to be impossible. First of all Jason had to harness a pair of fire-breathing bulls to a plough. Then he had to sow the tilled soil with the teeth of a famous dragon who had already been killed by another adventurer. But this was not the last of the dreadful tasks. Local people told Jason that as soon as he had sown the dragon's teeth a crop of armed men would spring up and attack him.

Despite the fact that he knew the tests would be physically impossible to achieve, Jason accepted both the terms and conditions because he had had an idea.

He went to the king's daughter, Medea, who was also a sorceress, and promised he would marry her if she used her magic to come to his aid. To convince Medea, Jason made his promise before the altar of the goddess Hecate. Delighted by his proposal, Medea agreed to help Jason, teaching him some spells that she promised would protect him from the bulls' fiery breath and the weapons of the crop of armed men. She also gave him an enchanted potion for further protection.

The next day, a huge crowd, including the uneasy Argonauts, arrived at the grove of Mars to watch what they were certain was going to be an impossible task. They were all sure Jason was going to die. He would either be trampled to death by the bulls, burned by their breath or killed by the armed men. The king took his place on the throne and thousands of other citizens of the kingdom of Colchis sat on the hillsides. Everyone waited, the tension rising.

Jason wondered if Medea's magic was going to work. She had seemed so confident. But just how powerful a sorceress was she?

Suddenly two enormous bulls thundered up, their hooves pawing

the ground, the fire from their nostrils burning up all the surrounding trees and foliage.

Jason stood his ground, but soon could hardly be seen as the smoke and flames surrounded him. The Argonauts chanted his name, sure that Jason stood no chance against the raging bulls. The crowd screamed in fearful delight while the king and his sorceress daughter looked on.

Jason saw Medea anxiously watching him through the flames, nodding her head as if to reassure him that her magical charm was going to work. *Have no fear.* Her words came into Jason's mind, calming him. *Have no fear.*

He strode calmly towards the bulls. Ignoring the burning breath he patted their necks and then quietly slipped the yoke over their monstrous heads. Leading them firmly forward, he made them drag the plough.

The Argonauts shouted with joy and the Colchians were amazed. How had Jason survived the fiery breath of the bulls? Why hadn't he been burned to a crisp?

Medea smiled encouragingly as Jason began the second task – sowing the dragon's teeth and ploughing them in. For a while there was silence as the bulls and their plough finally came to rest.

No one spoke. Time seemed to have come to a grinding halt. Then, without warning, the magical crop that Jason had sown only minutes before began to grow. Slowly, yard by yard, an army of men rose from the ground. Together they turned towards Jason, brandishing their weapons, preparing to attack him.

He glanced at Medea and saw that she was pale with fear. Did she doubt the strength of her spell? The army seemed very large and the Argonauts wondered if the test was going to be too much for Jason.

At first Jason kept the men at bay with a sword and shield. But he

knew he was soon going to be beaten as the dragon's-teeth army began to advance on him. He refused to give in and the Argonauts thought they had never seen one man fight so ferociously and with such passion. Medea waited. Why didn't Jason do what she had told him? Had he forgotten, or was he just leaving it until too late?

Although he knew it could leave him momentarily vulnerable, Jason realized that he had to use the spell. Lowering his shield, he seized a stone and threw it into the middle of the army. To his intense relief, within seconds, the men began to fight amongst themselves. Amazingly, the warriors hacked each other to pieces until there was not a single survivor left.

The Argonauts ran to embrace Jason, and Medea would have done the same if she had dared. But her father had no idea about their love for each other. If he had, he would have put Jason to death immediately. Medea had to stand quietly by the king's side.

But the tests were still not over. The dragon who never slept still stood between Jason and the Golden Fleece. The young adventurer had another magical battle on his hands and had never felt so exhausted.

Despairingly he looked up at Medea and she nodded again, silently reminding him that her magical powers would see him through. Immediately Jason remembered the enchanted potion – he had begun to think it would never be used.

Jason walked slowly towards the huge and scaly dragon that he knew could kill him with one blow, despite his sword and shield.

The dragon's eyes were huge and almost hypnotic as it glared at Jason. Nevertheless he kept on walking until he was in range. Then he scattered a few drops of the potion over the dragon who was now standing up on his hind legs and roaring at his potential victim. As the potion entered his huge round eyes, the dragon stood for a moment completely motionless. Then he keeled slowly over, falling into deep sleep for the first time in his life.

The dragon overcome, Jason grabbed the Golden Fleece from

inside the grove of trees, slung it over his shoulder and slowly approached the king's throne to the renewed cheers of the Argonauts. There he gazed deep into Medea's eyes.

She knew what he meant. This was the time. The time to run away together, back to the ship. For a moment she hesitated. She knew her father would do everything he could to stop her running away with Jason, directing his army to kill them both.

Jason knew that not a moment could be lost. He beckoned to the Argonauts and gave them a whispered command.

The king looked puzzled, not understanding what was going on.

Then Jason grabbed Medea's hand. Still carrying the Golden Fleece and surrounded by his faithful crew, he began to run back to the ship with Medea.

Ætes was furious and ordered his men to chase and arrest them.

But Jason and his Argonauts were too fast, running towards the harbor with such speed they became a blur, as if a storm cloud were racing along the ground.

Eventually they reached the *Argo*, jumped aboard and began to row back to Thessaly, taking another route along the coast. The ship streaked along with Medea and Jason gazing back at the hazy shoreline of the kingdom of Colchis, the Golden Fleece still safely slung over Jason's shoulders.

PEOPLE AND PLACES IN GREEK MYTHS AND LEGENDS

ARIADNE The daughter of King Minos of Crete. She helped Theseus to escape from the Labyrinth after he had killed the Minotaur. Although he took her with him when he left Crete, Theseus later abandoned her on the island of Naxos.

ATHENE The goddess of wisdom and the daughter of Zeus, king of the gods. Athene had no mother and she was born, fully formed as an adult, from her father's head.

ELYSIAN FIELDS The place where good spirits of the dead lived, following judgement in the Underworld. If their thoughts and actions in the upper world had been bad they were condemned to suffer in the fires of Tartarus.

THE GOLDEN FLEECE This came from a magical ram, sent by Hermes to save two children who were in danger from their stepmother. Unfortunately the girl, Helle, fell off the back of the ram as it flew over the strip of sea that divides Europe and Asia. It was named Hellespont after her and is now known as the Dardanelles. The ram was more successful with the boy, Phryxus (*frick*-suss), and was able to put him down safely in the Kingdom of Colchis where he was kindly received by King Æetes. Phryxus sacrificed the ram to Zeus and gave the Golden Fleece to the king in gratitude for his help.

HADES The king of the Underworld.

HECATE The goddess of black magic. Hecate lived in the Underworld and was also the queen of ghostly spirits. Sometimes she emerged into the upper world where she could be found lurking at lonely crossroads.

HEPHAESTUS The son of Zeus and Hera, the king and queen of the gods. Hephaestus was in charge of all practical work that needed doing in Olympus.

HERMES The messenger of the gods. Hermes possessed a pair of winged sandals so that he could carry out his tasks more quickly.

LABYRINTH A building containing many winding passages where it is very easy to get lost. The famous Labyrinth of Crete was built by Daedalus to contain the Minotaur. Each year, seven Athenian boys and girls were fed to this monster, which had a bull's body and a human head. No one dared to enter the Labyrinth to kill it because they were afraid they would never find their way out. Theseus eventually managed to destroy the Minotaur and escaped with the help of King Minos's daughter Ariadne, who gave him a ball of thread to guide him out again.

MUSES The goddesses of poetry, music, drama and science. They were led by Apollo who was the god of the sun, music, poetry and medicine.

OLYMPUS A mountain in northern Greece, believed to be the home of the gods. The Ancient Greeks believed that the Earth was disc-shaped, and that Greece was at the center of the disc. Olympus was said to be at the exact center of Greece.

PERSEPHONE The daughter of Demeter, goddess of the Earth. Hades fell in love with Persephone and carried her away to the Underworld. Demeter pleaded with Zeus to intervene, and he agreed to send Hermes to collect her. But she was only allowed to return for half the year. It was believed that autumn and winter came when Demeter was grieving for her daughter, and spring and summer came when Persephone returned to the upper world and Demeter was happy again.

THRACE A country to the west of the Black Sea and south of the Balkan mountains. In ancient times, it was inhabited by a warlike people who were also noted for their poetry and music.

TITANS The gigantic offspring of Father Sky and Mother Earth. The Titans were the first human beings to be created by Chaos, god of the unformed Earth. Some of the most famous gods and goddesses of Greek mythology, such as Zeus and Hera, were the children of the Titans. There was a great battle between the Titans and the gods from which the gods emerged victorious.

TROY Troy was a legendary city, said to be in modern Turkey. The Trojan War, between the Greeks and the people of Troy, lasted for ten years. The Greek poet Homer told the story of the war in his poem the *Iliad*.

UNDERWORLD In Greek mythology, the place filled with the spirits of dead mortals. Some were being punished for sins against the gods; others lived more peacefully in happier surroundings. Very rarely, the living were allowed to pass through on a mission. The Underworld was also filled with demons, giants and monsters who had opposed the gods and were busy producing creatures even more unpleasant than themselves.

PRONUNCIATION GUIDE

(stress the parts of the word in italics):

Ætes (ay-*eet*-eez)

Ariadne (ar-ee-*ad*-nee)

Aristaeus (arist-*ay*-uss)

Athene (a-*thee*-nee)

Cassiopeia (cass-ee-oh-*pay*-ah)

Cisthene (siss-*thee*-nee)

Daedalus (*day*-dal-uss)

Danaë (*dan*-ah-ay)

Epimetheus (epi-*meeth*-ee-uss)

Eurydice (yoo-*rid*-ee-see)

Euxine (*yook*-sine)

Graeae (*gray*-eye)

Hades (*hay*-deez)

Hecate (*hek*-at-ee)

Hephaestus (hef-*ay*-stuss)

Hermes (*hur*-meez)

Medea (med-*ee*-ah)

Orpheus (*or*-fee-uss)

Pasiphaë (par-*siff*-ah-ay)

Pangaeum (pan-*gay*-um)

Persephone (purss-*eff*-oh-nee)

Perseus (*purss*-yooss)

Phineus (*fin*-yooss)

Polydectes (pol-ee-*dek*-teez)

Prometheus (prom-*eeth*-yooss)

Theseus (*theess*-yooss)

Zeus (z-*yooss*)

INDEX